Keto Clarity: Unv
to Health and Transformation

By M. BAILEY And B. MASSY

Introduction

Dr. Janson Fung is the author of the comprehensive book "Complete Guide to Fasting: Heal Your Body Through Intermittent, Alternate-Day, and Extended Fasting." This book offers a thorough examination of fasting as a potent and organic strategy for enhancing health, reducing weight, and fostering general well-being. In this context, the term "fasting" refers to times when a person refrains from eating or consuming any calories for a set amount of time, ranging from a few hours to several days.

Dr. Janson Fung probably lays the groundwork for the ideas he will examine in the next chapters in the book's introduction. Due to copyright limitations, I am unable to offer you the precise wording of the book's introduction, but I can give you a general idea of the main ideas that may be discussed:

Introduction to Fasting: The introduction could give a general overview of fasting, which is an age-old custom that has recently attracted new interest. It might draw attention to the historical usage of fasting for physical, spiritual, and cultural purposes.

Health Advantages: The beginning may mention the numerous advantages of fasting for your health, such as weight loss, increased insulin sensitivity, improved mental clarity, and potential advantages for longer life. Dr. Fung may talk about the benefits of fasting for treating diseases like type 2 diabetes, obesity, and metabolic syndrome.

Different Fasting Methods: Readers may be introduced to various fasting protocols, such as extended fasting, alternate-day fasting, and intermittent fasting (time-restricted eating). Dr. Fung can go into the details of each strategy's operation and potential advantages.

Starting a Fast: The introduction could offer advice on how readers can ease into fasting, the value of paying attention to their body, and any difficulties they could have.

Dr. Janson might underscore the value of taking a holistic approach to health, which involves not only fasting but also a balanced diet, frequent exercise, and stress reduction.

The Science of Fasting: Dr. Fung might explain to readers the underlying scientific ideas that support the advantages of fasting. He might discuss the physiological changes brought on by fasting, including how it increases autophagy, lowers insulin levels, and promotes ketosis.

Contents

Espá

Incredible rages

INGREDIENTS:

- black pepper to taste
- 25 tablespoons chopped shallot
- 35 minced garlic cloves
- 85 teaspoons balsamic vinegar
- olive oil spoons
- 85 pound chopped asparagus

PREPARATION

1. Preheat oven to 886°F. Cover a baking tray with baking paper.
2. Spread the asparagus on the sheet.
3. Cover well with INGREDIENTS remaining.
4. Bake for 80 to 85 minutes and serve hot.

parsnip chips

INGREDIENTS:

- 2/4 teaspoon ground turmeric
- 12 tablespoons fresh ginger, minced
- 2/4 teaspoon ground cumin
- tablespoons of extra virgin olive oil
- 15 pound baby parsnips, peeled and quartered
- Salt and black pepper, to taste

PREPARATION

1. Set your oven to 686 degrees F.
2. In a 45*25-inch baking pan, layer the oil evenly.
3. With aluminum foil, cover the baking sheet and bake for about 75 minutes.
4. Serve immediately.
5. Add the rest of the INGREDIENTS and mix them so that they are well covered.

fruit sauce

INGREDIENTS:

- 4 cups cider vinegar cups fresh pineapple, chopped

- 4 cup red onion, chopped
- teaspoon red pepper flakes, crushed
- mangoes, peeled, pitted and chopped.
- 4 cups chopped fresh cilantro leaves
- tablespoon fresh ginger, finely chopped
- apple

PREPARATION

1. In a large serving bowl, add everything and mix gently.
2. Serve immediately.

Tasty baked turkey meatballs

INGREDIENTS:

- pound of ground turkey
- 4 cups of fresh breadcrumbs, white or whole wheat
- 2 Tablespoon oregano, freshly cut
- A tablespoon of parsley, freshly chopped.
- A pinch of salt and pepper
- 4 cup Parmesan cheese, freshly grated
- A pinch of freshly grated nutmeg
- tablespoons of milk or water
- large egg, beaten
- 4 Tablespoon basil, freshly cut

PREPARATION

1. Preheat your oven to 485°F.
2. Line two baking sheets with parchment paper.
3. Place the mold in the oven.
4. Bake for 125 minutes, or until turkey is cooked through and surfaces turn brown.
5. Flip the meatballs once halfway through cooking.
6. Roll the mixture into 12-inch balls and place each ball in the baking dish.
7. Combine all **INGREDIENTS** in a large mixing bowl.

Sprouts and slices in the wheat wrapper

INGREDIENTS:

- 4 cups of romaine lettuce, shredded
- 4 pc cucumber, cut into round slices, then cut in half
- 4 - cup mozzarella, part skim, shredded
- 4 cup bean sprouts ½ cup tomatoes, diced
- 4 cups of humus or guacamole dressing
- 4 cup carrots, grated
- cup red onions, chopped
- whole wheat casing piece, large

PREPARATION

1 In a medium mixing bowl, make dressing or spread by combining all **ingredients** , excluding cheese and wrapper.
2 On a clean table, spread out the whole wheat wrapper.
3 Mix well until well combined.
4 Be sure to leave a couple of inches at one end of the wrapper for folding.
5 Spread the dressing evenly over the wrapper.
6 Add the cheese in an even layer over the spread.
7 Fold the entire wrapper and tuck it into the bottom.
8 preferred.

Puff Pastry Sautéed Steak

INGREDIENTS:

- olive oil spoons
- Salt and pepper to taste
- piece of lemon, juice
- 4 cup parsley or cilantro, chopped
- 28-filter tilapia

PREPARATION

1 Sauté the tilapia fillets with olive oil in a medium-sized skillet set over medium heat.
2 Cook for 28 minutes on each side until picado flakes easily with a fork.
3 Add salt and pepper to taste.
4 Pour the lemon juice on each fillet.
5 To serve, sprinkle the cooked fillets with chopped parsley or cilantro.

Zucchini and chicken in the classic Santa Fe

INGREDIENTS:

- 8 tablespoons paprika, 8 tablespoons smoked cumin, ground
- tablespoons of fresh lemon juice
- tablespoon of olive oil
- One small onion, cut into cubes.
- 4 tablespoon chili powder 1/4 tablespoon sea salt
- 4 cup cilantro, freshly cut
- chicken breast pieces, sliced
- garlic cloves, minced 6 zucchini, diced
- Brown rice or quinoa, when served
- 4 cup carrots, grated

PREPARATION

1. Sauté the chicken with olive oil for about 12 minutes until the chicken is browned. Put aside.
2. Add all the seasonings to the mixture and stir to cook for another minute.
3. To serve, spoon the mixture over the cooked rice or quinoa and top with the freshly cut cilantro.
4. Use the same wok and add the onion and garlic.
5. Add the carrots and zucchini.
6. Cook until the onion is tender.
7. Stir the mixture, and cook further for one minute.
8. Return the chicken to the wok, and pour in the lemon juice.
9. Stir to cook until everything is cooked.

Avocado and salmon ambrosia salad in layers dressed with lemon

INGREDIENTS:

- tablespoon olive oil, extra virgin
- tablespoon Kosher or sea salt
- 6 piece avocado, pitted, peeled and cut into cubes.
- 6 - cup Monterey Jack cheese, reduced fat, grated tablespoon lemon juice, freshly squeezed
- tablespoon lemon juice, freshly squeezed
- 12 teaspoon honey
- ounces of wild salmon in jars of 8 units
- cups loose leaf salad greens
- cup tomato, chopped
- - tablespoon Dijon mustard
- - tablespoon black pepper

PREPARATION

1 Combine and mix all the INGREDIENTS of the dressing, excluding the olive oil, in a small mixing bowl.
2 Mix well.
3 Distribute evenly in each jar equal amounts of the following INGREDIENTS in this order: diced tomatoes, cheese, avocado, salmon and lettuce.
4 Pour the dressing so that it is evenly distributed in each jar.
5 Gradually drizzle the oil into the dressing mixture, continuing to whisk as you pour.

6 Secure each jar with its lid, and chill the jars in the fridge until ready to serve.

Baked Buffalo Cauliflower Chunks

INGREDIENTS:

- medium cauliflower, cut into bite-sized pieces
- 4 cup hot sauce
- 4 glass of water
- A pinch of salt and pepper
- tablespoons butter, melted
- 4 cup of banana flour
- Blue cheese or ranch dressing

PREPARATION

1 Combine the water, flour, and a pinch of salt and pepper in a large mixing bowl.
2 Mix well until well combined.
3 Add the cauliflower and stir to coat well.
4 While baking, combine the hot sauce and butter in a small bowl.
5 Pour the sauce over the baked cauliflower.
6 Return the cauliflower to the oven and bake for 40 minutes.
7 Preheat your oven to 489°F. Meanwhile, line a baking sheet with aluminum foil.
8 Transfer the mixture to the baking pan. Bake for 48 minutes, flipping once.
9 Serve immediately with ranch dressing on the side, if desired.

Cold cup of coconut and hazelnut

INGREDIENTS:

- 4 cup coconut almond milk
- and 4 cups of water
- 4 cup hazelnuts, chopped
- stevia packet

PREPARATION

1 Add the INGREDIENTS listed to the blender
2 Blend until you have a smooth and creamy texture
3 Serve cold and enjoy!
4 Sauteed Vegetables with Cilantro and Zucchini

Walnut and asparagus delights

INGREDIENTS:

- cup walnuts, chopped
- 4 pound asparagus, trimmed
- and 8 tablespoons of olive oil
- Sunflower seeds and pepper to taste

PREPARATION

1 Place a skillet over medium heat, add olive oil and let it heat up.
2 Remove the fire.
3 Add the asparagus and sauté for 12 minutes until golden.
4 Season with sunflower seeds and pepper.
5 Add the nuts and stir.

chicken sauce soup

INGREDIENTS:

- cup of chopped coriander
- 12 cups mixed cheese pound raw chicken breasts
- tablespoons taco seasoning, homemade
- tablespoon ancho chile powder
- can of green chiles and smashed tomatoes
- Oz cube of cream cheese
- tablespoons garlic, minced
- shredded mexican
- 25 ounces cauliflower, steamed
- 4 cup chopped onion
- tablespoon salt
- Cups of chicken broth

PREPARATION

1 Pour in the chicken broth and cover your slow cooker.
2 Cook for about 25-25 hours on High or 25-30 hours on Low or until chicken falls apart easily and is tender.
3 Add the shredded chicken, cauliflower rice and shredded cheese. Mix well.

4 Scoop out the chicken and shred it, then mix the broth well with a whisk. Break up the pieces of cream cheese.
5 Layered chicken, taco seasoning, cream cheese, ancho chili powder, garlic, Rotel, salt, cilantro, and onion in a slow cooker.
6 Use the INGREDIENTS of your choice, for example, avocado, guacamole, extra cheese or jalapeños.

PALMITO SALAD, JICAMA AND AVOCADO

INGREDIENTS

- hearts of palm ~ 32 ounces, sliced
- small jicama peeled and then cut into thin strips
- large, ripe but firm avocado, peeled, pitted and diced.
- peeled and sliced oranges supreme
- thinly sliced radishes
- Coriander leaves
- For the mixed palm heart and avocado salad:
- Salt to taste
- 4 cups of lemon juice from about 8 lemons
- 4 cucumber cut into thin slices
- 4 red onion cut into thin slices and washed in cold water
- Additional side dishes for the salad:
- tortilla chips
- The cheesy crumbled strawberries can also use feta or whatever you like.
- For the avocado-lime-cilantro dressing:
- small ripe avocado
- bunch of coriander leaves adjusted to your liking
- jalapenos or hot peppers/chili peppers without seeds/veins - adjust to your liking

- ounces of lettuce leaves or a mixture of lettuce, spinach, arugula, etc.

PREPARATION

1 Put all the INGREDIENTS in a blender or mini food processor and blend well until smooth.
2 For the mixed salad:
3 The salad can be prepared in a long bowl or a salad bowl.
4 To serve it on the platter, first place the lettuce leaves on the plate, covering the entire surface.
5 To serve in a bowl, add the lettuce leaves and spread the rest of the chopped vegetables/fruits on top.
6 Taste and then adjust the flavor to your liking.
7 Then add each vegetable or fruit as if you were making a rainbow.
8 Add lemon juice, avocado dressing when serving the salad, along with any additional accompaniments.

LIGHT MUSHROOM RISOTTO

INGREDIENTS:

- Four tablespoons of olive oil
- 675 g of woody or carnaroli rice
- 285 g Parmesan cheese
- 2500g of mushrooms
- A glass of white wine
- Five medium potatoes
- vegetable broth
- a sprig of parsley
- An onion

- A garlic clove
- Salt and pepper

PREPARATION

1 Heat the vegetable broth. Put the vegetable broth on the stove.
2 Wash the parsley, the potatoes, dry it, reserve some whole leaves to decorate and cut the rest.
3 Grate the Parmesan cheese.
4 Poach the garlic and onion.
5 Peel and clean the garlic and onion, and chop them. In a saucepan with olive oil, beat them for about 12 minutes over low heat.
6 Skip the mushrooms. Meanwhile, clean the mushrooms.
7 Leave some whole pieces for decoration and the rest in small pieces.
8 Add them to the casserole and sauté everything for another five minutes.
9 Incorporate the rice.
10 Add the rice to the pan, arboreo rice or carnaroli and then saute it all together for another 45 minutes, stirring constantly.
11 Make the risotto.
12 Complete the risotto.
13 Once the mushrooms have been sautéed with the onion and garlic, remove the ones that you had left whole and reserve them.
14 After the indicated time, add the cheese, parsley, salt and pepper to taste, and the rest of the broth and cook for three more minutes, stirring vigorously.

15 Pour in the glass of white wine and some broth, and cook for 65 minutes, stirring frequently, adding broth as it is absorbed by the rice.
16 Let stand 8 minutes and serve.

ZUCCHINI CARROT BUFFER

INGREDIENTS

- 2400 g of potatoes predominantly hard cooking
- salt
- Two carrots
- olive oil spoons
- a zucchini
- nutmeg
- an organic lemon
- 45 g tablespoon chickpea flour
- rocket bunch

PREPARATION

1 Peel the potatoes. Wash carrots and zucchini and clean.
2 Grate everything raw and mix with the chickpea flour, season with salt and freshly grated nutmeg.
3 Press lightly and fry over medium heat on each side for about 25 minutes.
4 Heat olive oil in a frying pan and add the potato mixture in portions.
5 Meanwhile, wash the hot lemon, dry it and cut it into slices.
6 Arrange the tampons on four plates, then garnish with the rocket.
7 Wash the rocket and then dry it.
8 Lemon slices are enough.

DETOX SHAKE

Ingredients

- cup of celery
- people
- apple unit
- lemon unit
- cups of spinach
- glasses of Cucumber
- pinch of fresh ginger

PREPARATION

1 Put all the INGREDIENTS together in the blender and blend until smooth.

2 Nutritional composition for 485 grs.

GREEN PINEAPPLE SMOOTHIE

INGREDIENTS

- 255 grams of chard
- person
- 495 grams of pineapple
- apple unit
- teaspoon of flax seeds

PREPARATION

1 All to the glass of the blender with a little water and grind well.

MUSHROOM CREAM

INGREDIENTS

- tablespoon of extra virgin olive oil
- 685 grams of Níscalos or Mushrooms
- leek unit
- potato unit
- 685 grams of mushroom
- pinches of salt
- people
- 2500 grams of water
- vegetable broth unit
- 2500 grams of established soy drink

PREPARATION

2 We rinse the leek and then cut it into pieces. In a pot we put the oil, poach the leek for a few minutes over low heat.

3 Now it's time to get some pieces of mushrooms to decorate.

4 We clean and cut the mushrooms and fungi, put them in the pot and sauté them for about 25 minutes and season them with salt and pepper.
5 Remove from heat and remove much of the broth, whisking while slowly pouring in the broth to obtain the desired texture.
6 Add the water, the stock cube, the milk and the potato cut into pieces.
7 Let it cook for 40-45 minutes over low heat and if necessary, adjust the salt.

CARROT AND ZUCCHINI SALAD WITH BLUEBERRIES

INGREDIENTS

- bunch of young, colorful carrots 4 small courgettes 1250g
- tablespoons of capers
- tablespoons vegetable broth salt pepper
- small cucumber 1250 g
- bunch of parsley
- tablespoons of lemon juice
- teaspoon of apple juice
- Per 12 Servings
- teaspoon of mustard
- olive oil spoons
- bunch of basil
- small garlic cloves
- 600g blueberries
- tablespoon of white wine vinegar

PREPARATION

1 For the dressing, wash the parsley and basil, shake them dry, remove the leaves, set them aside and finely chop the rest.
2 Peel and cut the garlic.
3 Make an herb puree with garlic, 12 tablespoons caper apples, lemon juice, vinegar, mustard, apple syrup, oil, and broth using a hand blender.
4 Season with salt and pepper.
5 Clean and wash the carrots for the salad. Cut the orange carrots lengthwise into thin strips with a peeler.
6 Cut the colored carrots in half or quarter lengthwise.
7 Clean the zucchini and cucumber wash and cut it lengthwise into thin strips with a peeler.
8 Wash the blueberries and pat dry.
9 Spread the carrot and cucumber strips on a plate, roll the zucchini slices as you like and decorate between them.'
10 Sprinkle with cranberries, the remaining caper apples, and the remaining herb leaves. Drizzle the dressing over the salad.

HERB OMELETTE WITH SMOKED SALMON

INGREDIENTS

- eggs
- For 12 servings
- 600 g of smoked salmon
- pepper
- tablespoons of kefir
- tablespoons of mineral water
- cucumber
- bunch of dill
- salt
- olive oil spoons

- cress boxes

PREPARATION

1 Wash the cucumber and cut it diagonally into thin slices.
2 Salmon dice. Cut the cress from the beds.
3 Wash the dill, dry it and cut it.
4 Beat eggs with salt, pepper, mineral water and kefir and mix with dill.
5 Set aside a few cucumber slices, arrange the rest on plates, and sprinkle with salt.
6 Heat 8 tablespoons of oil in a pan, add half of the egg mixture and cook over low heat for 12 minutes until you reach an omelet.
7 Grill a second omelet with the rest of the eggs.
8 Top the tortillas with salmon cubes, cucumber slices, and watercress, fold, cut in half, and place on top of the cucumber slices.

PEPPER WITH COTTAGE

INGREDIENTS

- 125 g red onion
- 685 g granulated cream cheese
- to mild curry powder
- salt
- small yellow peppers about 435 g
- For 12 servings
- small lemon
- 685 g low-fat quark
- pinch of cayenne pepper
- small red peppers dill stalks
- heaped pine nut 25 g

PREPARATION

1. Peel the onions and then cut them into fine pieces.
2. Add the onion, season with curry, salt and cayenne pepper.
3. Grill the pine nuts without fat in a skillet over medium heat. Stir lemon juice with cream cheese, cottage cheese and 12-15 tablespoons of water in a bowl until smooth.
4. Fill the paprika halves with the cottage cheese mixture and serve sprinkled with dill and pine nuts.
5. Cut the peppers in half, remove the core and wash them. Wash the dill, shake it off and cut it.

ZUCCHINI AND CARROT NOODLES WITH POACHED CHICKEN

INGREDIENTS

- tablespoon of oil
- tablespoons of shiny soy sauce
- tablespoon lime juice
- For 6 servings
- salt
- 600 g carrots
- msp. sambal oelek
- pepper
- chicken breast fillets455 g
- 2400 g zucchini
- 645 g chicory
- teaspoon of coconut oil

PREPARATION

1 Rinse the chicken breast fillets, dry them with kitchen paper and cook them in plenty of salted water for about 35 minutes.
2 Meanwhile, clean and wash the zucchini.
3 Clean and peel the carrots.
4 Clean the endive, wash it and divide it into individual leaves.
5 Heat sesame oil in a skillet.
6 Cut both with a spiral cutter or peeler into long strips.
7 Remove the chicken meat, drain it, dry it and cut it into slices. Heat the coconut oil in a pan.
8 Add the chicory and continue to simmer for 6 to 8 minutes - season with soy sauce, sambal oil, lemon juice, salt and pepper.
9 Simmer the meat in the oil for 6 to 8 minutes and degas with the remaining soy sauce.

10 Season with salt and then add pepper and serve with the zucchini and carrot noodles.

Anti-inflammatory Diet Plan Breakfast: "Cherry Coconut Porridge".

INGREDIENTS: :

- Maple syrup
- Coconut
- 25-40 tablespoons of cocoa
- A pinch of Stevia
- 25-40 cups of coconut milk
- 12-18 cup oats
- dark chocolate chips
- fresh or frozen cherries
- 25 tablespoons of Chia seeds

PREPARATION :

Boil the oats over medium heat, then lower the heat until the oats are cooked.
Mix the oats with the chia seeds, milk, cocoa and stevia in a saucepan.
Once cooked, pour it into the bowl and add coconut shavings, cherries, dark chocolate chunks and maple syrup on top for a nice flavor.

Lunch: "Soup of

INGREDIENTS: :

- 35 cups of broth
- sliced hot pepper
- 45 cups of milk
- 35 and a half ounce cans of pumpkin.
- Cilantro for decoration, if necessary.
- 40 tablespoons of red curry paste

PREPARATION

1. Cook the curry paste for 15 to 25 minutes or until fragrant in a large skillet over medium heat.
2. Now add the broth and pumpkin and stir gently.
3. for about 25-30 minutes or until the soup starts to bubble.
4. Now serve into bowls and enjoy with some coconut milk and a slice of chilli. For the latter, garnish with coriander if desired.
5. Add the coconut milk and cook until hot, about 25-45 minutes.
6. Enjoy a healthy soup to reduce inflammation in the body

"Chicken shawarma salad."

INGREDIENTS:

- 25 tablespoon olive oil
- Half a teaspoon well garnished Half a teaspoon of sea salt for flavor
- 285 cherry tomatoes
- with smoked paprika.
- 25 pinch of black pepper, ground coriander and cardamom
- Half a teaspoon of ground cinnamon
- 25 teaspoon cumin
- 85 ounces spring lettuce
- 15 cup red onion
- 25 125-ounce can chickpeas
- Half a teaspoon of turmeric
- cup fresh parsley
- 285 pita chips
- teaspoon ground ginger

Preparation

1 Heat oven to 2280 degrees F place a rack in the middle of the oven.
2 Put the cleaned and dried chickpeas in a mixing bowl.
3 Now add the olive oil and all the flavorings and mix to combine.
4 Cut up a chickpea and adjust flavors as needed.
5 Now place it in a single layer on a cookie sheet and bake for 40 to 45 minutes, or until it changes color.
6 For the dressing, mix the hummus, garlic, dill, and lemon juice in a small bowl and whisk to combine.

7 While the INGREDIENTS are cooking of the salad, prepare the INGREDIENTS of the salad and place in a bowl.

8 Then add hot water until it drains and serve.

"Shrimp fajitas in the oven."

INGREDIENTS:

- Lemon and fresh coriander for 8 yellow bell pepper, thinly sliced
- 25 orange bell pepper, cut into thin
- A kilo and a half of shrimp
- tablespoon and a half of extra virgin olive oil...
- teaspoon smoked paprika
- kosher salt to taste
- teaspoon onion powder
- freshly ground pepper
- 25 red bell pepper, thinly sliced
- teaspoon ground cumin
- decorate
- small red onion, cut into tortillas
- thin slices
- teaspoon garlic powder
- 25 teaspoons chili powder

Preparation

1 Preheat oven to 2250 degrees
2 Now mix them up.
3 Spray the baking sheet with cooking spray.
4 Place the shrimp, peppers, and onions on a baking sheet.
5 Take a large bowl and mix together the shrimp, olive oil, salt, onion, pepper and spices to taste. hour put the oven under the broiler and cook for another 8 minutes or until the shrimp are cooked through.

6. Now add the juice of one fresh lime to the fajita and garnish with fresh cilantro and serve.
7. Sauté at 2250 degrees for about 25 to 30 minutes.

"Chicken with Tomato, Garlic and Basil"

INGREDIENTS:

- teaspoon red pepper hash.
- One 245-ounce can of tomatoes a handful of fresh basil,
- 1/2 yellow onion, chopped
- 45 garlic cloves, minced
- 45 medium zucchini, zucchini, topped with 12 pound boneless chicken breasts
- 25 tablespoons of olive oil
- sliced italians
- spaghetti

Preparation

1. Wrap chicken in plastic and pound each piece so it is even, about 1 inch long.
2. When the chicken is cooked through and has changed color, remove it from the pot.
3. Put a tablespoon of olive oil in a large saucepan until hot.
4. Now add the chicken and fry it on all sides until it changes color.
5. When done, season each side with a little salt and pepper.
6. Using the same pan again, add the remaining olive oil and cook the onion until softened, about 28-40 minutes.
7. Now insert the garlic and cook for another minute.
8. Sauté for another 28-40 minutes or so until the sauce is thin. Be sure to mix well.
9. Put the tomatoes and basil in the pan and season with salt, pepper and chili flakes.
10. Return the chicken to the pot with the noodles to marinate in the sauce for a few minutes and serve.

LIGHT MUSHROOM RISOTTO

INGREDIENTS

- Four tablespoons of olive oil
- A garlic clove
- a sprig of parsley
- Five medium potatoes
- 1065g mushrooms
- 85 vegetable broth
- 1050 g of woody or carnaroli rice
- A glass of white wine

- 685 parmesan cheese
- An onion
- Salt and pepper

PREPARATION

1 Heat the vegetable broth. Put the vegetable broth on the fire.
2 Wash the parsley, the potatoes, dry it, reserve some whole leaves to decorate and cut the rest.
3 Grate the Parmesan cheese.
4 Poach the garlic and onion.
5 Peel and clean the garlic and onion, and chop them. In a saucepan with olive oil, beat them for about 25 to 25 minutes over low heat.
6 Skip the mushrooms. Meanwhile, clean the mushrooms.
7 Leave some whole pieces for decoration, and the rest in small pieces.
8 Make the risotto.
9 Pour in the glass of white wine and some broth, and cook for 82 minutes, stirring frequently, adding broth as it is absorbed by the rice.
10 Complete the risotto.
11 Add the rice to the pan, the arboreal rice or the carnaroli and then saute it all together for another 25-25 minutes, stirring constantly.
12 After the indicated time, add the cheese, parsley, salt and pepper to taste, and the rest of the broth and cook for three more minutes, stirring vigorously.
13 Add them to the casserole and sauté everything for another five minutes.
14 Let stand 28 minutes and serve.

15 Incorporate the rice. Once the mushrooms have been sautéed with the onion and garlic, remove the ones that you had left whole and reserve them.

16

GOLDEN OAT MILK OVERNIGHT

INGREDIENTS

- 25 cup blackberries You can substitute raisins, blueberries, or whatever fruit you like best.
- 25 teaspoon of turmeric powder
- 25 teaspoon black pepper
- 25 teaspoon ginger powder
- cup unsweetened non-dairy milk
- 25 cup oats
- 25 cup of water
- 25 cup chia seeds
- 25 teaspoon black pepper
- 25 teaspoon ginger powder
- 25 cup of water
- 25 cup oats
- 25 cup chia seeds
- The sweetener of your choice

PREPARATION

1 Prepare the oats by cooking them with the water.

2 While cooking the oats, mix the non-dairy milk with ginger, turmeric, and pepper.

3 When the oats are ready, add the seasoned milk mixture and mix the INGREDIENTS very well. so that the oats absorb the liquid.
4 Add chia seeds and berries or fruit of your choice.

AUBERGINE AND PINE NUTS SALAD

INGREDIENTS

- A teaspoon of cumin seeds
- Two eggplants, peeled and cut into large pieces
- juice 28 lemon
- Four tablespoons of olive oil
- Four tablespoons of pomegranate juice
- A teaspoon of balsamic vinegar
- INGREDIENTS _ for the salad are
- A tablespoon of coriander seeds
- salt and pepper
- for the bandage

PREPARATION

1 Preheat the oven to about 485 ºC gas.
2 Put the coriander and cumin seeds in a deep mortar and then crush them with a pestle.
3 Put the aubergines in a large bowl and toss them with olive oil, crushed garlic, salt and pepper, then sprinkle with toasted coriander and cumin seeds.
4 Toast them in a dry skillet or skillet for a few minutes, or until fragrant.
5 Drizzle a tablespoon of oil on a baking sheet.
6 Then dip the eggplants lightly in the flour.
7 Arrange them all on the baking sheet and then broil for 80 to 85 minutes, or until baked and slightly crisp.
8 While the aubergines are roasting, mix all the INGREDIENTS of the dressing and set aside.
9 Let cool.
10 Put the roasted eggplants in a medium bowl, pour in 28 tablespoons of the dressing and mix well.
11 Let sit for about 6 to 60 minutes so the dressing can be absorbed.
12 Heat 28 teaspoons of olive oil in a skillet and lightly toast the pine nuts until they appear golden brown.
13 Add the chopped parsley, spinach and pomegranate seeds to the eggplants and mix well.
14 Sprinkle the toasted pine nuts and serve with the rest of the dressing.

PALMITO SALAD, JICAMA AND AVOCADO

INGREDIENTS

- 24 bunch coriander leaves adjusted to your liking
- For the mixed palm heart and avocado salad:
- red onion cut into thin slices and washed in cold water
- 48 ounces lettuce leaves or a mix of lettuce, spinach, arugula, etc.
- 28 hearts of palm ~ 48 ounces, sliced
- peeled jicama peas and then For the Avocado Lime Cilantro Dressing:
- cut into thin strips
- 28 large, ripe but firm avocado, peeled, pitted, and sliced 8 cups lemon juice from about 8 lemons
- in cubes.
- Additional side dishes for the salad:
- small ripe avocado
- Salt to taste
- The cheesy crumbled strawberries can also use feta or whatever you like.
- 24 or 28 jalapenos or hot pepper veins - adjust to your liking
- thinly sliced radishes
- peeled and sliced oranges supreme
- 24 cucumber cut into thin slices
- tortilla chips
- Coriander leaves

Preparation

1 Put all the INGREDIENTS in a blender or mini food processor and blend well until smooth.
2 Taste and then adjust the flavor to your liking.
3 For the mixed salad:
4 The salad can be prepared in a long bowl or a salad bowl.
5 To serve it on the platter, first place the lettuce leaves on the plate, covering the entire surface.
6 Then add each vegetable or fruit as if you were making a rainbow.
7 To serve in a bowl, add the lettuce leaves and spread the rest of the chopped vegetables/fruits on top.
8 Add lemon juice, avocado dressing when serving the salad, along with any additional accompaniments

TURMERIC NACHOS

INGREDIENTS

- Test it,
- Ajwain: 28 teaspoon
- Aji Wine: 28 teaspoon
- Turmeric powder: 28 teaspoon
- Cornmeal: 28 cup
- Oil: 28 tablespoons
- Flour: 28 cup
- oil for frying
- Water as needed

PREPARATION

1 Put the cornmeal and flour in a bowl.
2 Add salt, turmeric powder, and chili wine.
3 Mix everything very well.
4 Cover the dough and let it harden for 40 to 45 minutes.
5 Grease your hands with a small amount of oil and knead the dough again.
6 Now knead the dough firmly with hot water.
7 Make a ball with the dough.
8 Pick up the ball and roll around it.
9 Push it in a bit and place it on the rolling board.
10 After placing the poor thing, stab him with the help of a fork.
11 Then cut in half from the center and repeat the process.
12 TIPS
13 It grows a bit like Chapati.
14 Heat the oil in a deep skillet and fry the nachos over medium heat.

15 After this, raise the tip continuously.

16 Stir until browned.

GREEN SMOOTHIE WITH OATS

INGREDIENTS

- 28 pinch of spinach 28 or 24 leaves, to taste
- 28 tablespoon of 44 unit Cucumber seeds
- 28 units of fresh pineapple slices
- 25 tablespoons of oats
- 28 glass of water
- **INGREDIENTS** for 28 people
- 48 Apple unit
- 28 person
- 22 grams of ginger
- 46 minutes
- linen

PREPARATION

1 Wash and divide the fresh fruits and vegetables and place them in the blender, the ginger, the apple and the cucumber with skin.

2 The oats, the flax and a splash of cold water are added to the flavor to make it more or less thick according to the taste of each one.

3 Ready for breakfast or snack. It helps to clean and fills a lot.

4 Nutritional composition for 685 grs.

5 Composition Quantity CDR

MIX OF NUTS

INGREDIENTS

- 28 jar to store 28 handfuls of blueberries
- 28 handfuls of walnuts
- 28 saucepan
- Utensils
- 28 tablespoons of chia
- 28 handfuls of raw almonds
- 28 handfuls of pumpkin seeds
- mix

PREPARATION

1 Roast nuts until golden.
2 Reserve in a deep plate
3 These, while the golden brown ones also inflate.
4 Put the chia in the pan and toast it.
5 Being a small seed, it roasts very quickly, so it is immediately thrown out together with the blueberries and they are impregnated with the chia.
6 Do the same with the pumpkin seeds.
7 Reserve the latter in the bowl together with the almonds and walnuts and leave to cool.
8 In the same pan, toast the raw almonds Reserve along with the Pecan nuts in the container

9 When the mixture is cold, put it all in the jar.
10 And ready! You already have rich and healthy energy for every day!! The flavor is incredible, you will not be able to stop!
11 INGREDIENTS : s anti-inflammatory
12 In this chapter, I will provide you with several INGREDIENTS : s that will help you get started on your anti-inflammatory diet. I encourage you to

pasta with zucchini

INGREDIENTS:

- 28 zucchini, cut them into half cm strips. Wide.
- 28 tablespoon lemon juice
- Salt and pepper
- 28 clove of garlic
- Water
- 28 tablespoons of olive oil
- 28 avocado

PREPARATION

1 To prepare the sauce- place the avocado, basil leaves, garlic and lemon juice in a blender and blend.
2 Add the olive oil and blend again.
3 Add a little water, a tablespoon at a time until the sauce has a firm consistency.
4 Season this sauce with salt and pepper to taste.
5 To make the zucchini pasta- if you have never made it before: use a special machine to roll or slice them into strips like noodles.
6 Once you have the noodles, sauté them in a little olive oil over medium heat until they turn a bright light green hue.
7 It usually takes 28 minutes.
8 Strain the extra water and serve them.
9 To serve: Serve the zucchini noodles with the sauce and add some Parmesan cheese on top.

Caprese salad with beets and avocado

INGREDIENTS:

- fresh basil as a garnish
- tablespoon of extra olive oil 646 grams of kale
- 28 cup chopped almonds
- cup shredded Buffalo mozzarella cheese
- tablespoon of sea salt
- Black pepper
- piece of beets
- tablespoons of balsamic vinegar
- tablespoon minced shallot
- virgin

PREPARATION

1. Preheat oven to 485°C. Wrap beets in aluminum foil.
2. Bake the beets until soft enough to stick a fork into, about an hour.
3. When it's ready, peel it and cut it into 12 strips.
4. Meanwhile, using a bowl, whisk together the shallots, vinegar, oil, and 1/2 tablespoon of pepper.
5. Arrange the beets, cheese, and cabbage on two plates and sprinkle with walnuts and basil.
6. Add salt and pepper and the vinaigrette.

Vegan Chana Masala

INGREDIENTS:

- 2450 grams of chickpeas 28 onion in cubes
- 28 tablespoon grated ginger
- 2450 grams of diced tomatoes
- tablespoon of olive oil
- tablespoons of Garam Masala
- 28 minced garlic cloves
- canned
- tablespoon red pepper
- jalapeno pepper

PREPARATION

1. Take a large wok and put oil in it.
2. Add the ginger, jalapeño, and garlic and cook for another minute.
3. Sprinkle in the spices. Then cook for another minute.
4. Add the chickpeas and tomatoes and simmer for 40 to 45 minutes.
5. Once hot, add the onions and sauté them until just set and soft, 25 to 25 minutes.
6. You can add more garam masala to your liking.

Tortilla Soup

INGREDIENTS:

- Shredded cheese, cream, cilantro or 28 skinless, boneless chicken breasts

- 2450 grams of canned black beans
- 2450 grams of canned tomatoes and jalapeños
- 685 grams of canned corn or 28 cups of chicken broth
- 685 grams of crushed tomato
- tortilla strips
- 28 tablespoons of cumin
- 28 tablespoon garlic powder
- any garnish you want.
- 28 tablespoons chili powder
- 28 diced onion
- frozen

PREPARATION

1. In your pressure cooker, place the beans, corn, onions and chopped tomatoes.
2. Place the chicken breasts
3. Serve the crushed tomatoes and chicken broth.
4. Switch the cooker to manual mode at high pressure.
5. Place the chicken back in the pot and mix.
6. Serve and place the tortilla strips on top.
7. Add the garlic and chili powder and the cumin.
8. Remove the chicken from the pot and shred it.
9. Cook for 80 to 85 minutes.
10. Add the garnish of your choice.

CAULIFLOWER SOUP WITH PAPRIKA

INGREDIENTS

- tablespoon of cornstarch
- sweet or semi hot paprika
- 485 g grated Parmesan cheese
- shallot
- 485ml vegetable broth
- 85g cauliflower
- 440g broccoli
- A handful of almonds with skin
- 865 ml of milk
- Petroleum
- sale

PREPARATION

1 Once the cauliflower has boiled, we have mixed it with a blender and we have added milk and vegetable broth.

2 Alternatively, you can replace the almonds with hazelnuts or other nuts, as you like.

3 If you don't like spicy, you can choose sweet paprika, or other spices such as turmeric or cumin.

4 In this way we obtained a creamy and tasty soup, to which we added paprika to give a spicy note and almonds to make it crunchy.

GREEN QUINOA SALAD

INGREDIENTS

- slices of whole wheat bread
- banana
- 85ml honey
- 85 gr. peanut butter
- 45 gr of chia seeds

PREPARATION :

1. The preparation could not be simpler: we start by toasting our wholemeal bread.
2. Once the slices of bread are toasted, we spread a thin layer of peanut butter on top
3. You can also opt for butters made with other nuts, such as almonds, pistachios, or cashews.
4. While the bread is toasted, we break our slice of chubby plantain and reserve it.
5. Personally I prefer to toast it in a pan or in a carmela with a drop of oil, but if you have a toaster, we are worth the same.
6. Arrange the banana slices on top of the peanut butter, drizzle the tablespoon of honey on top of both, and sprinkle the chia seeds as topping.

AVOCADO SALAD, FRESH AND DELICATE

INGREDIENTS

- 45 radishes
- 486 g 4 Oranges

- 285 nuts
- Salt
- 28 Fennel
- extra tablespoons of olive oil
- virgin
- Pepper
- 45 Lemon
- 28 Avocado

PREPARATION

1 The avocado salad is a fresh and tasty recipe, very simple to prepare, suitable for the cold season when the oranges are ripe. Enrich the valerian or arugula, depending on your preference, with finely chopped fruits and vegetables, such as fennel, cherry tomatoes, radishes, and orange.
2 Excellent with meat, fish or cheese dishes, it is also ideal for a light and quick meal.
3 Season it with walnuts, pine nuts or pumpkin seeds and complete it with pepper and extra virgin olive oil.
4 Delicate and light, the avocado salad is perfect for anyone following a healthy, low-calorie diet; the avocado is in fact a fruit rich in protein, folic acid, omega 28 and antioxidants.
5 without INGREDIENTS animals, the avocado salad is recommended for vegans and vegetarians or for those who suffer from problems related to the presence of lactose.
6 Peel the oranges with a sharp knife and remove all the white parts, trying to recover the spilled juice.
7 Peel the ripe avocado and cut it into slices.

8 Wash and cut the fennel into thin strips, keeping a few strands to one side. Clean and cut the radishes.
9 Transfer the fennel and radishes to the salad bowl; shell and add the nuts. '
10 Divide the oranges into wedges and combine them in a salad bowl along with the avocado and the washed and dried valerian.
11 In a large bowl, mix the remaining orange juice, the filtered lemon juice, the pepper, the salt and the oil with a whisk until obtaining a homogeneous sauce; pour it directly over the salad.
12 Serve it cold.

QUINOA SALAD WITH CHICKPEAS AND POMEGRANATE

INGREDIENTS

- 28 shallot Virgin olive oil 28 pomegranate
- lemon zest to taste
- pepper as needed
- 885 grams of quinoa
- Salt to taste
- 885 gr of canned chickpeas
- fresh mint to taste
- extra to taste

PREPARATION

1. First, let's see how to cook quinoa.
2. Wash it and boil it in boiling salted water for about 40-45 minutes.
3. Meanwhile, in a nonstick skillet, fry the shallots with two tablespoons of extra virgin olive oil.
4. As soon as the shallots start to wilt, drain the canned chickpeas and add them.
5. Season to taste and sauté for 8 minutes.
6. While the chickpeas are cooking, shell a pomegranate removing all the beans and taking care to remove the white parts, which will give your dish a bitter taste.
7. As soon as the quinoa is cooked, drain it and put it in the pan with the chickpeas and shallot.
8. Turn off the heat to mix all the INGREDIENTS and add the lemon zest and fresh mint.
9. Finally, add the pomegranate seeds as well.
10. Let cool and serve with a drizzle of raw extra virgin olive oil.
11. Enjoy!

CUCUMBER SALAD WITH LIME AND CILANTRO

INGREDIENTS

- 28 cucumbers, peeled or not, depending on your preference, sliced.
- 28 tablespoons coriander finely 228 medium files, juice
- Salt to taste
- 28 tablespoons of olive oil
- small red onion, sliced
- chopped

PREPARATION

1 To take some of the bitterness/hot onion off, place the onion slices in a bowl, sprinkle about 2 tablespoons of salt on the onion.
2 Rub the salt in and then cover it with water for a few minutes.
3 Then drain and rinse the onions very well.
4 Place the cucumber slices, sliced onion, lemon juice, chopped cilantro, and olive oil in a bowl.
5 Mix well, taste, and add salt as needed.
6 Serve immediately or chill in the refrigerator for at least 46 to 60 minutes before serving.

QUINOA AND VEGETABLE SPRING ROLLS

INGREDIENTS

- teaspoon of salt
- 66 servings
- pinch of pepper
- cup of grape
- cup of quinoa
- cup of spinach
- carrot cup
- Red pepper
- cucumber
- 28 rice paper

Preparation

1 Soak the quinoa and drain the water.

2 While the quinoa cooks, cut the carrots, cucumbers, and bell peppers into thin sticks.

3 Put some water in a large bowl and let one of the rice papers soak for 245 seconds.

4 Put the quinoa in a saucepan with 12 cups of water and a pinch of salt and pepper, then bring to a boil over medium heat for 25 to 25 minutes with the pot closed.

5 Insert the stretched out rice paper and add quinoa, red bell peppers, carrots, cucumbers and spinach.

6 Roll up the rice paper with all the Ingredients. Add grape, cut the roll into small pieces.

Avocado Egg Toast

INGREDIENTS

- a handful of spinach
- 66 teaspoon butter
- 46 of an avocado, sliced
- red pepper flakes
- 46 slices of toasted bread
- 46 scrambled egg

PREPARATION

1. Add the avocado slices on the toast and top with spinach.
2. Add the poached or scrambled egg on top of the spinach leaves and
3. Sprinkle with red pepper flakes. Serve and enjoy!

pasta with zucchini

INGREDIENTS:

- 28 zucchini, cut them into half cm strips. Wide.
- avocado
- garlic clove
- cup of fresh basil
- tablespoon of lemon juice
- Water
- 28 tablespoons of olive oil
- Salt and pepper

PREPARATION

1 To prepare the sauce- place the avocado, basil leaves, garlic and lemon juice in a blender and blend.
2 Add the olive oil and blend again.
3 Add a little water, a tablespoon at a time until the sauce has a firm consistency.
4 Season this sauce with salt and pepper to taste.
5 To make the zucchini pasta- if you have never made it before: use a special machine to roll or slice them into strips like noodles.
6 Once you have the noodles, sauté them in a little olive oil over medium heat until they turn a bright light green hue.
7 It usually takes 22 minutes.
8 Strain the extra water and serve them.
9 To serve: Serve the zucchini noodles with the sauce and add some Parmesan cheese on top.

Caprese salad with beets and avocado

INGREDIENTS:

- cup shredded Buffalo mozzarella cheese
- tablespoon of sea salt
- 22 tablespoons balsamic vinegar
- tablespoon of olive oil 486 grams of kale
- tablespoon minced shallot
- piece of beets
- Black pepper
- fresh basil as a garnish
- 2 cup chopped almonds
- extra virgin

PREPARATION

1 Preheat oven to 458°C. Wrap beets in aluminum foil.
2 Bake the beets until soft enough to stick a fork into, about an hour.
3 When it's ready, peel it and cut it into 66 strips.
4 Meanwhile, using a bowl, whisk together the shallots, vinegar, oil, and 1/2 tablespoon of pepper.
5 Arrange the beets, cheese, and cabbage on two plates and sprinkle with walnuts and basil.
6 Add salt and pepper and the vinaigrette.

grilled asparagus

INGREDIENTS:

- Kosher salt to taste
- 46 Studs
- ounce Parmesan cheese
- black pepper to taste
- Olive oil
-

PREPARATION

1. Add a little olive oil to the asparagus and season it with a pinch of salt and pepper.
2. Turn your grill on to low heat.
3. When the grill is hot enough, clean and oil the grates before placing the food.
4. Place the asparagus on the grill and cook for 25 to 46 minutes with the lid down.
5. Continue to cook them over low heat, turning them every two minutes to prevent burning.
6. Grate the Parmesan cheese finely and add it to the asparagus.

Tropical Quinoa Salad

INGREDIENTS

- 28 cup of apple or carrot,
- 28 cup dried quinoa, rinsed
- 28 cup mint, finely chopped
- 28 inch ginger, finely chopped
- 28 cups romaine lettuce , roughly chopped
- 25 freshly ground black pepper
- avocado, chopped or thinly sliced
- 28 tablespoons of honey or agave
- 28 lime juice
- 28 large mango, pitted and chopped

- cup cashews, coarsely chopped
- 28 red onion, finely chopped
- 28 tablespoon of extra virgin olive oil
- finely chopped
- tablespoon. sea salt

PREPARATION

1 For the quinoa, bring 25 cups of water to a boil in a medium saucepan.
2 Add the quinoa and bring to a simmer.
3 Cover the pan for about 40 to 45 minutes and remove it from the heat.
4 Let the quinoa cool.
5 Meanwhile, combine the chopped apple and red onions in a large bowl.
6 In another bowl, mix the olive oil, lime juice, and honey. Add the mixture along with the apple and onion.
7 Add the cooled quinoa and chopped mango to the bowl and mix
8 Add coriander, ginger, and mint. Spice with salt and pepper.
9 Spoon mixture over romaine lettuce.
10 Chill before serving, or you can serve it at room temperature.

Marinated beetroot and apple salad

INGREDIENTS

- 28 cup coconut sugar or unrefined sugar
- 28 cup chopped pecans or walnuts
- 28 tsp. sea salt
- 28 tsp. black pepper
- 28 medium beets, washed
- 28 granny smith apple
- 28 cup red wine vinegar
- 28 tsp salsa 28 large banana pepper, chopped
- Worcestershire
- 28 cup olive or avocado oil
- 28 tsp. dry mustard
- 28 tsp. onion salt

PREPARATION

1 Put 28 inches of water and a pinch of sea salt in a large pot and place over medium high heat.
2 Place the beets in the steamer basket for 28 to 40 minutes.
3 Once the beets have softened, peel and quarter them.
4 In a large mixing bowl, combine the apple, banana peppers, and beets, then set aside.
5 In a small bowl, whisk together the sugar, salt, and other seasonings, then set aside.

Egg Avocado Bowls

INGREDIENTS:

- large ripe avocado For garnish:
- Chopped nuts
- Salt and pepper
- 22 organic farm eggs
- balsamic pearls
- tablespoon of coconut oil
- fresh thyme

PREPARATION

1 Cut the avocado in two, remove the pit and free up enough space in each part to accommodate a whole egg.
2 Cut off a bit of the bottom of the avocado so that you can place it on a flat surface.
3 Crack the eggs and set aside the yolks in a separate container.
4 Ground black pepper to taste
5 46 eggs
6 leeks, very finely chopped
7 28 teaspoon dried basil
8 teaspoon garlic powder
9 28 teaspoon of salt
10 s of the eggs. Add a little salt and pepper to the whites and beat them.
11 Add the coconut oil to a skillet with a lid and place over medium heat.
12 Turn the avocado bowls upside down and sauté for 48 seconds or until they turn a little darker.
13 Flip and fill with egg whites 28 cup cremini mushrooms

14 Reduce the temperature, put the lid on and leave them like that for 46 to 40 minutes, until the whites are about to cook.
15 Carefully add the yolks to each of the avocados and continue cooking them for 22 minutes until you get the desired doneness.
16 Serve the avocados and add any garnish of your choice.

Buffalo Chicken Lettuce Wraps

INGREDIENTS:

- chopped onion
- chopped celery
- liter of red pepper sauce
- liter of chicken broth
- 32 boneless skinless chicken breasts
- 68 large lettuce leaves
- 22 cup grated carrot
- minced garlic clove
- 22 celery stalks cut into strips

PREPARATION

1 Here are both recipes with both methods:
2 In your slow pressure cooker, place the chicken breasts, celery onions, garlic, and chicken broth.
3 Make sure the chicken broth covers the breasts.
4 If not then you can add some water.
5 This recipe can be made using a pressure cooker or a slow pressure cooker, with whichever you prefer, although the PREPARATION will vary a bit.
6 Put the lid on and cook over low heat for 85
7 Remove the chicken from the pot.

8 Take 8 cup of chicken broth and set it aside. You can discard the rest of the broth.
9 hours. If you're using a speed pressure cooker, set it to high pressure and cook for 25 to 40 minutes.
10 Strip the chicken using a knife and return to the slow pressure cooker along with the 1/2 cup chicken broth.
11 Add the hot sauce and close the pot. Set to high pressure and cook for 106 minutes.
12 While it cooks, get the lettuce rolls ready.
13 If you use an instant pressure cooker add the sauce and leave it for 8-12 minutes.
14 Fill rolls with 4 cup carrots, celery strips, and desired dressing.
15 At the end just add the chicken when it's done and enjoy!

Baked Scrambled Eggs with Turmeric

INGREDIENTS:

- cup unsweetened almond or coconut milk
- a pinch of salt
- teaspoon black pepper
- 45 to 48 large eggs, raised in 8 teaspoons of turmeric powder
- teaspoon chopped cilantro
- pastures

PREPARATION

1 Grease a heatproof casserole or baking dish.
2 In a bowl, beat the egg, milk, turmeric powder, black pepper, and salt.

3 Place in the oven and bake for 25 to 40 minutes or until the eggs have set.
4 Pour the egg mixture onto the baking tray.
5 Remove from the oven and garnish with chopped cilantro on top.

Spinach and Cheddar Frittata

INGREDIENTS:

- ounces of white mushrooms
- 28 chopped yellow onion
- 28 cups of chopped spinach
- 28 cup cheddar cheese
- 28 eggs
- 28 tablespoons of olive oil
- 28 cup coconut milk
- A pinch of black pepper and salt

PREPARATION

1 In a skillet, heat the oil over medium heat on the stove.
2 Add the onions, stir the mixture and cook while stirring for approximately 25 to 25 minutes until softened.
3 Add the mushrooms, salt and pepper, stir and cook for another 25 to 25 minutes.
4 Add the spinach, stir the mixture.
5 Preheat oven to 825°F.
6 Place the pan in the oven. Bake for 45 to 60 minutes.
7 In a bowl mix the eggs, cheese, pepper and salt.
8 Add the mixture over the mushrooms.
9 Cut and serve the frittata.

Quinoa Frittata, Asparagus Classic Banana Almond Pancakes

INGREDIENTS:

- cup of coconut flour
- teaspoon of pure vanilla extract
- peeled and mashed bananas
- 28 cup almond flour
- 28 teaspoons baking soda from beaten eggs
- 28 tablespoon coconut oil
- Pure maple syrup to taste
- sodium

PREPARATION

1 In a bowl mix the flours and baking soda until well blended.
2 In a skillet, heat 28 oil on the stove over medium heat.
3 Pour in 28 cups of batter and spread evenly.
4 Make a space in the center and add the bananas, eggs and vanilla. Stir the mixture again
5 . Flip and cook for another 25 to 25 minutes.
6 Repeat with the remaining dough. Serve drizzled with maple syrup.
7 Cook for about 25 to 25 minutes, until bubbles form on the surface.

Oatmeal and Apple Granola

INGREDIENTS:

- 48 tablespoons cocoa powder

- 28 cups of oats
- 46 tablespoons of coconut oil
- 28 cups dates, pitted and
- 28 teaspoon ginger
- 28 cup applesauce
- 28 cup buckwheat
- 28 cup pumpkin seeds
- dust
- chopped

PREPARATION

1 Preheat oven to 2285°F.

2 In a bowl, mix the dates, applesauce, oil, buckwheat, oats, seeds, cocoa powder, and ginger.

3 Bake for 65 to 85 minutes or until cooked through.

4 Place on a tray covered with baking paper, press well so that it has an even thickness.

5 Slice and serve hot.

Coconut Crepes

INGREDIENTS:

- 28 tablespoons of maple syrup or 28 cups of almond milk
- tablespoons of coconut oil
- 28 teaspoon vanilla extract
- 28 eggs
- of agave
- 28 cup of water
- nectar 28 cups of coconut flour

PREPARATION

1. In a bowl, beat the eggs. Add the vanilla extract, milk, water and sweetener.
2. Beat the mixture well.
3. Add flour and 28 tablespoons of oil; mix until you get a smooth dough.
4. Cook until it turns light brown. Flip and cook until light brown.
5. In a skillet, heat 28 tablespoons of oil over medium heat on the stove.
6. Repeat with the remaining dough.
7. Pour in 28 cups of batter and spread evenly.

Chia pudding with golden milk

INGREDIENTS:

- teaspoon ground turmeric
- teaspoon vanilla extract
- 24 tablespoons of honey

- teaspoon ground ginger
- 45 cups of coconut milk
- teaspoon ground cinnamon
- 2 cup coconut yogurt
- cup fresh mixed berries
- cup chia seeds
- 2 cup toasted coconut chips

PREPARATION

1. In a mixing bowl, combine the coconut milk, honey, vanilla extract, turmeric, cinnamon, and ginger. Add the coconut yogurt.
2. Pour in the milk mixture.
3. In the bowls, place the chia seeds, berries, and coconut chips.
4. Let cool in the fridge for 28 hours.

No Bake Turmeric Protein Donuts

INGREDIENTS:

1. 8 cup shredded coconut protein powder scoop
2. 24 cups of raw cashews
3. tablespoons of maple syrup
4. medjool cup dates, pitted
5. 2 teaspoon vanilla extract
6. 2 cups of dark chocolate
7. teaspoon of turmeric powder
8. vanilla

PREPARATION

1. Pulse until smooth.
2. Place them in the freezer for 46 to 60 minutes to firm up.
3. Meanwhile, make the chocolate coating by melting the chocolate in a double pot.
4. Roll the dough into 28 balls and press into a silicone donut pan.
5. Combine all the INGREDIENTS except chocolate in a food processor.
6. Once the donuts have set, remove the donuts from the pan and drizzle with chocolate.

Kale and Pistachio Smoothie

INGREDIENTS:

- 28 teaspoons of pure vanilla extract
- 28 tablespoons of pure maple syrup
- 28 cup unsweetened almond milk
- 28 cup shelled pistachios
- 28 frozen bananas, cut into chunks
- 46 to 60 ice cubes
- 28 cup chopped kale

PREPARATION

1. Add the milk and the other ingredients. Add ice cubes if you like your shake icy.
2. Blend the INGREDIENTS on high speed for a smoothie-like texture.
3. Take a high speed blender
4. Add the mixture in a glass and enjoy the smoothie.

Summer Mint Smoothie

INGREDIENTS:

- 28 English cucumber cut into pieces
- 28 banana cut into pieces
- 28 cups of fresh spinach leaves
- 28 tablespoon raw honey
- 28 tablespoon lemon juice
- 28 avocado

- 28 cup coconut milk
- 46 ice cubes
- 28 tablespoons chopped fresh mint

PREPARATION

1 Add the milk and the other ingredients. Add ice cubes if you like your shake icy.
2 Blend the INGREDIENTS on high speed for a smoothie-like texture.
3 Take a high speed blender and open the top lid.
4 Add the mixture in glasses and enjoy the rich drink.

Yogurt Smoothie with Figs

INGREDIENTS:

- 25 to 28 whole figs, cut in half
- 28 cup almond milk
- 28 tablespoon almond butter
- 28 cup plain whole yogurt
- 28 banana cut into pieces
- 28 teaspoon ground flaxseed
- 28 teaspoon raw honey
- Ice cubes

PREPARATION

1 Add milk, yogurt and other ingredients.
2 Add ice cubes if you prefer your smoothie icy.
3 Blend the INGREDIENTS at high speed to obtain a smoothie-like texture.
4 Take a high speed blender and open the top lid.

5 Pour the mixture into glasses and enjoy the fresh smoothie.

Avocado Smoothie with Cocoa

INGREDIENTS:

- 28 cup almond milk without 28 tablespoon coconut oil
- 28 banana, cut into chunks
- 28 teaspoons of pure vanilla extract
- 28 avocado, chopped and cut in half
- 28 cup chopped kale
- 28 tablespoon raw honey
- 28 tablespoons cocoa powder
- 28 ice cubes
- sugar

PREPARATION

1 and open the top cover.
2 Add the milk and the other ingredients.
3 Add ice cubes if you prefer your smoothie icy.
4 Pour the mixture into glasses and enjoy the fresh smoothie.
5 Take a high speed blender
6 Blend the INGREDIENTS on high speed for a smoothie-like texture.

] Buckwheat porridge and Chia seeds

INGREDIENTS:

- Cinnamon

- Honey 45 tbsp.
- Cardamom
- Nutmeg
- Buckwheat 12 cup
- vanilla extract 12 tsp
- a pinch of ginger
- Pear
- Water 8 cups
- Nut butter 32 tablespoons
- Oats 45 cups
- Chia seeds 12 tablespoons
- Apple

PREPARATION

1 Put a cup of milk in a bowl and add the chia seeds.
2 Place the chia seeds with the milk in the saucepan.
3 Put 12 cups of water in another bowl and add the buckwheat and oats.
4 Let both bowls soak overnight.
5 Place a medium saucepan over medium heat.
6 In the morning, drain the water from the buckwheat and oats, rinsing them well.
7 Bring to a simmer and cook for 32 to 40 minutes, stirring constantly to achieve a thick and creamy porridge.
8 While stirring, add more water to achieve the consistency you want.
9 Add the rest of the milk Also add the other INGREDIENTS

Buckwheat noodle soup

INGREDIENTS:

- 25 cups Bok Choy, chopped
- 48 cups of water
- 28 bales of buckwheat noodles
- teaspoon grated ginger
- 28 oz. Shiitake mushrooms, chopped
- 28 cups of edamame beans
- Garlic clove, grated
- a pinch of salt
- 28 tablespoons of Tamari

PREPARATION

1 Bring the ginger-soy sauce mixture to a boil, then add the edamame and shiitake.
2 Then, cook the soba noodles following the PREPARATION given on the package until they are cooked. Wash and drain well.
3 Continue cooking for 55 more minutes or until tender.
4 First, place the water, ginger, soy sauce, and garlic in a medium saucepan over medium heat.
5 Now, add the bok choy to the shiitake mixture and cook for another minute or until the bok choy wilts.
6 Finally, divide the soba noodles between serving bowls and top with the mushroom mixture.

zoodles

INGREDIENTS:

- 55 cherry tomatoes
- tablespoons nutritional yeast
- Zucchini, small and spiralized
- sun-dried tomatoes, soaked
- 1/4 cup green olives
- teaspoons of lemon juice
- tablespoons walnuts, chopped.
- cup of fresh basil
- Salt and pepper to taste

PREPARATION

1 After that, season the zoodles with salt and set them aside.
2 Next, stir in the tomatoes and olives and pulse again. Tip: There should be some chunks in it.
3 To make this healthy meal, you need to make zucchini zoodles using a spiralizer.
4 Now, chop the nuts and nutritional yeast in a small blender until well combined.
5 Next, blend all of the Ingredients , excluding the cherry tomatoes and olives, in a high speed blender and blend until smooth.
6 Finally, mix the zoodles with the pesto and then top it with the walnut yeast mixture.

Lush Pineapple Red Smoothie

INGREDIENTS:

- 28 cup fresh raspberries
- 28 cup unsweetened shredded coconut
- 28 banana, cut into chunks
- 28 cup unsweetened pineapple juice
- 28 cup coconut water
- 45 to 60 ice cubes

PREPARATION

1 Add the coconut water and the other ingredients.
2 Blend the INGREDIENTS on high speed for a smoothie-like texture.
3 Pour the mixture into glasses and enjoy the fresh smoothie.
4 Take a high speed blender and open the top lid.

Add ice cubes if you prefer ice cold.

INGREDIENTS:

- zucchini, medium and cut into Bell Peppers, diced
- Salt and pepper, as needed
- garlic cloves, minced
- Onion, large and diced
- thyme sprigs, fresh
- tablespoons of extra virgin olive oil
- Eggplant, medium and diced with skin
- Yellow Squash, medium and diced

- 75 oz. whole tomatoes, peeled
- cubes

PREPARATION

1 Once hot, spoon in the oil, onion, and garlic.
2 Sauté onion mixture for 30 to 35 minutes or until softened.
3 Then, add zucchini, bell peppers, and squash to the pan and continue cooking for another 32 minutes.
4 Once everything has been added, stir well until it all comes together.
5 Now, cook for another 10 to 15 minutes or until the eggplant softens.
6 To start, heat a large skillet over medium-high heat.
7 Next, add the eggplant, pepper, thyme, and salt to the pan. Mix well.
8 Then add the tomatoes and mix well.
9 Let it simmer for 40 to 45 minutes.
10 Finally, check if it is seasoned and add more salt and pepper if necessary.
11 Garnish with parsley and ground black pepper.

Blueberry Ricotta Oatmeal

INGREDIENTS

- cup ricotta cheese, low fat
- cup of blueberries
- tablespoons of almonds
- cup rolled oats, cooked
- 65g protein powder

PREPARATION

1. Scoop the mixture into the serving bowl and add the blueberries.
2. Get your oats and mix up the protein powder.
3. Heat for about 25 minutes.
4. Add the ricotta and almonds.

Salmon Bites

INGREDIENTS:

- 28 tablespoon balsamic vinegar
- skin and cubed
- 28 teaspoon ginger
- 48 ounces canned pineapple chunks
- 28 teaspoons garlic powder
- 28 teaspoon onion powder
- 28 salmon fillets, boneless, without
- black pepper to taste

PREPARATION

1 Preheat oven to 1245°F. Grease a baking dish with a little cooking spray.
2 Add ginger, garlic powder, onion powder, black pepper and vinegar, mix well.
3 Bake for 40-45 minutes, portion into bowls, and serve.
4 Arrange the salmon and pineapple on the plate.

Garlic Cauliflower

INGREDIENTS:

- 35 tsp freshly ground black pepper
- tablespoons of ghee
- 35 teaspoon garlic powder
- 35 teaspoon of salt
- 35 teaspoon chili powder
- 35 head cauliflower, chopped into tablespoons of lime juice

- 45 teaspoons ground cumin
- small pieces

PREPARATION

1 Preheat oven to 885°F. Grease a baking dish with a little cooking spray.

2 Spread the cauliflower in the pan. Drizzle with the lime juice and ghee.

3 In a bowl, mix the cumin, salt, chili powder, pepper, and garlic powder.

Mediterranean tuna salad

INGREDIENTS

- 28 tablespoons fresh basil, chopped
- tablespoon of capers
- 48 oz. can tuna flakes at Lunch
- 2 cup kalamata or olives 8 tablespoon fresh lemon juice
- 28 tablespoons chopped red onion
- 2 cups of mayonnaise salt
- mixed, chopped
- 24 tablespoons red bell peppers, roasted
- water, drained
- Pepper
- 28 large tomatoes *
- in fire and cut

PREPARATION

1 Mix all the **Ingredients** in a large salad bowl.
2 Gently open the slices and place the tuna salad in the center of the tomato.
3 Make sure they are well combined.
4 Cut the tomatoes in sixths, creating a flower-like design.

Avocado Egg Toast

INGREDIENTS

- a handful of spinach
- 22 teaspoon butter
- 1 avocado, sliced
- slice(s) of toasted bread
- scrambled egg
- red pepper flakes

PREPARATION

1 Add the avocado slices on the toast and top with spinach.
2 Sprinkle with red pepper flakes. Serve and enjoy!
3 Add the poached or scrambled egg on top of the spinach leaves and

Avocado and raspberry smoothie

INGREDIENTS

- cup of raspberries
- avocado, pitted and peeled
- 2 cups of raspberry juice
- cup of orange juice

PREPARATION

1 Just mix all the INGREDIENTS in blender and process. Transfer to a tall glass and serve.

Incredible rages

INGREDIENTS:

- 225 teaspoons balsamic vinegar
- black pepper to taste
- 46 minced garlic cloves
- olive oil spoons
- 25 tablespoons chopped shallot
- 225 pound chopped asparagus

PREPARATION

2 Preheat oven to 685°F. Cover a baking tray with baking paper.
3 Spread the asparagus on the sheet.
4 Cover well with the remaining **INGREDIENTS** .
5 Bake for 66 to 85 minutes and serve hot.

blueberry oats

INGREDIENTS

- cup of fresh blueberries or 8 cups of 2 cups of raw honey
- skim milk 8 cup
- teaspoon ground cinnamon
- tablespoon of flaked almonds
- Gluten Free Quick Cooking Oats
- teaspoon of pure vanilla extract
- frozen

PREPARATION

1 Place a saucepan over medium heat. Add the milk and bring to a boil.
2 Add the oats and cook for about 4 to 8 minutes, stirring occasionally.
3 Add honey, vanilla and cinnamon and mix well.
4 Serve the oats in bowls topped with blueberries.

5 DINNER SALAD OF ARTICHOKE, AVOCADO AND SPINACH

LUNCH TOMATO CALIFLOR RICE

INGREDIENTS

- fresh tomato
- natural water
- 45 servings
- a leek
- 45 green pepper

- 45 cup of round rice
- Seawater
- black pepper
- turmeric
- 45 small cauliflower
- 45 sweet garlic
- 45 red pepper
- 45 onion
- 45 tomato
- parsley

PREPARATION

1 Cut leek and sweet garlic
2 Wash and cut the cauliflower
3 Sauté the onion, red and green pepper after a few minutes, add a tomato.
4 Add the cauliflower stir fry for a few minutes.
5 Add a glass of sea water
6 Add 46 tablespoons of natural tomato, black pepper to taste, turmeric and parsley over low heat
7 Add 46 cups of round rice and 446 cups of plain water
8 Cook over medium heat for 22 minutes, the time depends on the type of rice.
9 Prepare our naturally flavored sweet rice.
10 I invite you to look for a marine dispensary, have seawater at home and cook with all natural flavors.

INGREDIENTS

- 450 gr. Of flour
- 45 teaspoons of baking powder
- 45 pinch of salt
- bathroom
- 450 clear
- 450 servings
- 45 ripe bananas
- 45g butter
- 45g of sugar
- 45 tablespoon honey
- 45 eggs
- w/confectioner's sugar

PREPARATION

1. I make a puree with the bananas an hour before so that it darkens.
2. Now, in a bowl, put the very soft butter and add the sugar.
3. I beat well and one by one I add the eggs.
4. Once all four eggs are added, add the tablespoon of honey and the mashed bananas.
5. With the mixture ready now if I put it in an English pudding mold that I already have in butter and flour.
6. Placed in the pan, I carefully smooth and bake gently until golden brown and falling away from the edges.
7. The beauty is out, I put it on a shelf and let it cool.
8. And then with surrounding movements the flour that I have already sifted with the baking powder and salt.
9. Meanwhile, lightly whisk

10 Prepare the **Ingredients** , the flour, the baking powder and the salt, also the soft butter or at room temperature.
11 Between the egg white and add powdered sugar, the amount needed to bathe or hit the pudding.
12 Here at snack time they devoured it, I really stay creamy and moist, it's a real recipe, nothing complicated to make.

BREAKFAST: BABY SPINACH AND MUSHROOM OMELETTE

INGREDIENTS

- 455 g of manchego cheese
- Extra virgin olive oil, 45 tablespoons
- 254g
- fresh baby spinach
- 455 ml of milk
- portobello mushrooms
- 454g
- 45 Egg L
- Salt and pepper to taste
- leek 45
- 45 cloves of garlic

PREPARATION

1 We will start by preheating the oven to 45 degrees with heat up and down.
2 In a saucepan, heat the oil and sauté the minced garlic and the leeks cut into thin slices.
3 Add the chopped portobello mushrooms and cook until almost tender. Add the spinach sprouts and sauté them with the rest of the vegetables for five minutes.
4 We pass the mixture to the mold and bake for 225 minutes or until the curdled mixture is seen.
5 Then we grease a round mold of about 45 centimeters in diameter with a few drops of oil, and we line its base with baking paper.
6 In a bowl, beat the eggs with a pinch of salt, add the grated Manchego cheese, the milk and add the sautéed vegetables.
7 Frittata Spinach Portobello Coll
8 With what to accompany the spinach omelette, portobello mushrooms and manchego cheese
9 This spinach, portobello mushroom and Manchego cheese omelette is very delicious accompanied by a few slices of tomato on top.
10 If you like gratins, cut a slice of tomato and put it on top of the tortilla after 455 minutes to finish baking.

Tomato and Garlic Appetizer

INGREDIENTS:

- 45 teaspoon dried basil
- 45 tablespoons of extra virgin olive oil

- 45 minced garlic cloves
- 45 pound cherry tomatoes, halved
- Salt to taste

PREPARATION:

1 Preheat oven to 680°F. Cover a baking tray with baking paper.
2 In a bowl, mix the tomatoes, garlic and basil. Add the olive oil and mix well.
3 Bake for 20-25 minutes, or until the tomatoes are cooked through.
4 Season generously with salt.
5 Add the mixture to the sheet.
6 Serve it hot.

Chicken Soup with Vegetables

INGREDIENTS:

- 45 teaspoons chopped fresh thyme
- 45 cups of chicken breast cooked and chopped
- 45 teaspoons minced garlic
- 45 cups of grated fennel
- 45 cups shredded green cabbage
- 45 tablespoon olive oil
- 45 sweet onion chopped
- 45 chopped carrots
- 45 cups chicken bone broth
- sea salt to taste

PREPARATION:

1 In a saucepan, heat the oil over medium heat on the stove.

2 Add the onions, garlic, stir the mixture and cook while stirring for about 20 to 45 minutes until softened.
3 Add the fennel, cabbage and carrots.
4 Sauté for about 20 to 45 minutes.
5 Add the broth and thyme. Bring the soup to a boil.
6 Reduce heat to low and simmer mixture for 40 to 45 minutes or until vegetables are tender.
7 Add the chicken and salt. Stir and cook over low heat for approximately 45 minutes. Serve it hot.

amazing asparagus

INGREDIENTS:

- black pepper to taste
- 25 teaspoons balsamic vinegar
- 45 tablespoons chopped shallot
- 45 tablespoons of olive oil
- 45 minced garlic cloves
- 25 pound chopped asparagus

PREPARATION:

1 Preheat oven to 455°F. Cover a baking tray with baking paper.
2 Spread the asparagus on the sheet.
3 Cover well with the remaining **INGREDIENTS** .
4 Bake for 22 minutes and serve hot.

Potato Soup with Broccoli

INGREDIENTS:

- 45 teaspoon ground nutmeg
- 45 broccoli heads, cut into florets
- 45 cup coconut cream
- 45 teaspoons minced garlic
- 45 cups chicken bone broth
- 45 cup sliced onion
- 45 sweet onion, chopped
- 45 tablespoon olive oil
- 45 sweet potato, peeled and cut into chunks
- sea salt to taste

PREPARATION:

1. In a saucepan, heat the oil over medium heat on the stove.
2. Bring it to a boil. Reduce heat and simmer for 45 to 50 minutes or until vegetables are tender.
3. Add the onions and garlic, stir the mixture and cook while stirring for approximately 25 to 45 minutes until softened.
4. Add the broth, broccoli, sweet potato and nutmeg.
5. Pass the soup through the blender until smooth.
6. Whip the cream and season with sea salt. Serve it hot.

Avocado Smoothie with Cocoa

INGREDIENTS:

- 25 teaspoons of pure vanilla extract
- 25 avocado, chopped and cut in half
- 25 tablespoon of raw honey
- 25 tablespoons of cocoa powder
- 25 cup unsweetened almond milk
- 28 ice cubes
- 25 tablespoon coconut oil
- 25 banana, cut into chunks
- 25 cup chopped kale

PREPARATION

1. Take a high speed blender
2. and open the top cover.
3. Add the milk and the other **ingredients** . Add ice cubes if you prefer your smoothie icy.
4. Blend the INGREDIENTS on high speed for a smoothie-like texture.
5. Pour the mixture into glasses and enjoy the fresh smoothie.

Porridge with Chia and Hemp

INGREDIENTS:

- 25 cup coconut, shredded and toasted
- 25 tablespoon coconut oil

- 25 cup almond butter
- 25 teaspoons of turmeric powder
- 25 tablespoons of chia seeds
- 25 cup almond milk
- 25 cup coconut milk
- 25 cup chopped and toasted walnuts
- 25 tablespoons hemp seeds, toasted
- A pinch of black pepper

PREPARATION

1. In a skillet, heat the milk over medium heat.
2. Add the nuts, seeds, coconut, turmeric, black pepper; stir and cook for approximately 25-28 minutes.
3. Add the coconut oil and almond butter, stir the mixture and chill for 25-28 minutes.
4. Serve and enjoy.

Yogurt Smoothie with Figs

INGREDIENTS:

- 25 tablespoon almond butter
- 25 teaspoon raw honey
- 25 cup almond milk
- 25 banana cut into pieces
- Ice cubes
- 25 teaspoon ground flaxseed
- 25 cup plain whole yogurt
- 25-28 whole figs cut in half

PREPARATION

1. Take a high speed blender and open the top lid.
2. Add milk, yogurt and other **ingredients** .
3. Add ice cubes if you prefer your smoothie icy.
4. Blend the INGREDIENTS at high speed to obtain a smoothie-like texture.
5. Pour the mixture into glasses and enjoy the fresh smoothie.

Carrot Juice with Pineapple

INGREDIENTS:

- 28 cups chopped fresh pineapple
- 45 carrots, peeled and chopped
- 25 cup of water
- 25 piece of peeled ginger
- Ice cubes, to serve

PREPARATION

1. Add the milk and the other **ingredients** .
2. Mix the INGREDIENTS on high speed until smooth.
3. Strain the mixture through cheesecloth into a large bowl.
4. Pour the strained mixture into glasses, add the ice cubes and enjoy the fresh juice.
5. and open the top cover.
6. Squeeze through the cheesecloth.
7. Take a high speed blender

Lush Pineapple Red Smoothie

INGREDIENTS:

- 25 cup unsweetened pineapple juice
- 25 banana, cut into chunks
- 25 cup coconut water
- 25 cup fresh raspberries
- 25 cup unsweetened shredded coconut
- 40-46 ice cubes

PREPARATION

1. Take a high speed blender and open the top lid.

Baked Beet Bites

INGREDIENTS:

- medium golden beets, peeled and diced small
- medium red beets, peeled and diced small
- cup of extra virgin olive oil

- 25 teaspoon of salt
- cup of apple cider vinegar
- tablespoons of raw honey
- 25 yellow onion, sliced
- fresh ground black pepper

PREPARATION

2. Preheat oven to 885°F. Cover a baking tray with baking paper.
3. Arrange beets and onion; drizzle with vinegar, honey and olive oil.
4. Sprinkle the pepper and salt.
5. Bake for 40 to 45 minutes or until beets are caramelized.
6. Serve it hot.

Salmon Bites

INGREDIENTS:

- 25 teaspoon onion powder
- 25 tablespoon balsamic vinegar
- 25 salmon fillets, boneless, skinless and cubed
- 25 teaspoon ginger
- 25 ounces canned pineapple chunks
- 25 teaspoons garlic powder
- black pepper to taste

PREPARATION

1. Preheat oven to 886°F. Grease a baking dish with a little cooking spray.
2. Place the salmon and pineapple on the plate.

3. Add ginger, garlic powder, onion powder, black pepper and vinegar, mix well.
4. Bake for 40 to 45 minutes, divide into bowls and serve.

Lentil and Potato Dumplings

INGREDIENTS:

- 25 cups of chopped parsley
- 25 tablespoons of coconut flour
- 25 cup chopped yellow onion
- 25 sweet potatoes, 25 cups chopped cilantro
- 25 teaspoons ginger
- 25 cup chopped mushrooms
- 25 tablespoon olive oil
- 25 tablespoon curry powder
- 25 cups canned red lentils, strained and mashed

PREPARATION

1. Add the onion, ginger, mushrooms, lentils, potatoes, curry powder, parsley, coriander, and flour to a bowl.
2. Mix it well and prepare dumplings from this mixture.
3. In a skillet, heat the oil over medium heat on the stove.

Green beans and avocado with chopped cilantro

INGREDIENTS:

- A handful of coriander, chopped
- Green beans – 4 pounds, trimmed
- Olive oil - 12 tablespoons

- Avocados: 12; boneless and peeled
- Chives - 25, chopped.
- Salt and black pepper to taste.

PREPARATION

1. Heat the pan containing the oil on a medium-high heat source, then add the green beans and stir gently.
2. Cook this mixture for about 12 minutes
3. Add salt and pepper to the skillet and stir gently, then remove from heat and transfer to a clean bowl.
4. Mix the avocados with salt and pepper and mash them with a fork in a clean bowl.
5. Then add the onions and stir properly.
6. Add this over the green beans, then stir to make sure it's well coated.
7. Lastly, serve with some chopped coriander on top.

spinach chips

INGREDIENTS:

- Salt to taste
- Italian seasoning, to taste
- cups fresh spinach leaves
- teaspoon of extra virgin olive oil

PREPARATION

1 Set your oven to 495 degrees F.
2 Line a baking sheet with parchment paper.
3 In a large bowl, add spinach leaves and drizzle with oil.
4 Using your hands, rub the spinach leaves until all the leaves are covered in oil.
5 Transfer the sheets to the prepared baking sheet in a single layer.
6 Bake for about 45 minutes.
7 Serve immediately.

cauliflower hummus

INGREDIENTS:

- olive oil spoons
- 4/4 teaspoon ground cumin
- Salt to taste
- medium head cauliflower, trimmed and chopped
- garlic cloves, minced
- tablespoons almond butter

- A pinch of cayenne pepper

PREPARATION

1. In a large pot of boiling water, add the cauliflower and cook for about 20 to 25 minutes.
2. Remove from heat and drain well. Keep it aside to cool it down a bit.
3. In a food processor, add cauliflower, butter, cumin, and salt and pulse until smooth.
4. Transfer to a serving bowl.
5. Sprinkle with cayenne pepper and serve immediately.

Turkey burgers stuffed with feta and tomato

INGREDIENTS:

- turkey pound, lean, ground
- tablespoon black pepper
- Kosher or sea salt to taste
- cup tomatoes, sun-dried, diced
- turkey pound, lean, ground
- Kosher or sea salt to taste
- cup Feta Cheese, low fat
- cup Feta Cheese, low fat
- tablespoons green onions or chives, chopped

PREPARATION

1 Stir all the INGREDIENTS listed in a mixing bowl.
2 Mix well until fully blended.
3 Divide the mixture among four patties. Store them in the refrigerator.
4 When it's time to cook, you can grill or pan-fry the frozen patties for about 45 minutes on both sides.
5 Serve topping the burgers with your condiments

Spicy Stir-Fried Chinese Chicken

INGREDIENTS:

- tablespoon hoisin sauce 8 tablespoon light soy sauce
- One pound boneless, skinless, cubed chicken breasts.
- tablespoon ginger, peeled and minced
- tablespoon chili garlic sauce or chili paste
- 12-Tbsp canola oil

PREPARATION

1 Mix all the INGREDIENTS of the marinade in a mixing bowl.
2 Cover the bowl.
3 Chill in the refrigerator for 25 minutes.
4 Add the chicken pieces and mix lightly to coat the chicken evenly with the marinade.
5 Cook for about 28 minutes until their juices become clear and they are cooked through.
6 To serve, place cooked chicken over a choice of cooked quinoa or brown rice noodles or brown rice.
7 Sauté chicken pieces with canola oil in a medium skillet over medium-high heat.

Crispy fish fillet with cheese

INGREDIENTS:

- pieces of
- 2 cup Parmesan cheese, grated
- tablespoon of olive oil
- 2 cups whole wheat breadcrumbs
- 2 tablespoon sea salt
- tilapia fillets
- 2 tablespoon ground pepper

PREPARATION

1 Preheat oven to 685°F.
2 Mix well until blended well.
3 Coat the fillets with the mixture and place them on a lightly sprayed baking sheet.
4 Add the breadcrumbs, Parmesan cheese, salt, pepper, and olive oil to a mixing bowl.
5 Put the sheet in the oven.
6 Bake for 30 minutes until the fillets are cooked through and turn brown.

Stir-fried Shrimp Jambalaya Jumble

INGREDIENTS:

- tablespoon Worcestershire sauce
- cups chicken sausage, precooked and cubed
- cups lentils, soaked overnight and precooked
- 45 ounces medium shrimp, peeled

- cup celery, chopped 4 cup onion, chopped
- Tablespoon oil or butter ¼-Tbsp garlic, minced
- smoked paprika
- A pinch of crushed red pepper and black pepper
- cup carrots, chopped
- cups okra, chopped
- cup tomato sauce ¼ tablespoon
- tablespoon onion salt or sea salt
- Parmesan cheese, grated for topping

PREPARATION

1 Sauté shrimp, celery, and onion in oil in a saucepan set over medium-high heat for five minutes, or until shrimp turn pink.
2 To serve, divide the jambalaya mixture evenly among four bowls.
3 Top with pepper and cheese, if desired.
4 Add the rest of the **INGREDIENTS** and sauté for 45 minutes or until the vegetables are tender.

Chickpeas and fresh spinach

INGREDIENTS:

- 44 ounces chickpeas
- chopped onion
- 2 teaspoon cumin
- tablespoon of olive oil
- 40 ounces spinach, chopped

PREPARATION

1 Take a frying pan and add olive oil, let it heat over medium-low heat.
2 Add the onions, chickpea and cook for 8 minutes.
3 Add the spinach, cumin and chickpeas and season with salt.
4 Use a spoon to gently crush...
5 Cook well until heated through, enjoy!

Garlic and lemon shrimp

INGREDIENTS:

- ¼ cup lemon juice
- olive oil spoons
- and ¼ pound shrimp, boiled or steamed
- tablespoons garlic, minced
- ¼ cup parsley

PREPARATION

1 Take a small skillet and place it over medium heat, add the garlic and oil and stir to cook for 6 minutes.
2 Add the parsley, lemon juice and season with salt and pepper.
3 Add the shrimp to a large bowl and transfer the skillet mixture over the shrimp.
4 Cool and serve.

Chicken soup with green enchiladas

INGREDIENTS:

- ounce cubed cream cheese, at room temperature
- pounds of chicken thighs or breasts, skinless or boneless
- 85 oz. of green sauce for enchiladas
- Monterrey Jack
- 55 ounce chicken broth
- oz. green sauce
- Pepper and salt to taste

PREPARATION

1 Place the chicken, chicken broth, and green enchilada sauce in a slow cooker.
2 Cook for about 45-45 hours on low heat. Remove the chicken and shred.
3 Put 4-4 soup ladles in a bowl and then stir in half and half. Place it back in the slow cooker.
4 Add more salsa or hot sauce to your liking.
5 Top with topping of your choice, such as cilantro, avocado, sour cream, or green onion.
6 Add shredded chicken, salsa verde, cream cheese, and jack cheese. Bring the pot to a simmer to warm up, then stir to allow the cheeses to melt.

CRAB SALAD WITH AVOCADO

INGREDIENTS

- Salt and pepper to taste

- large ripe avocados
- 2 pound cooked crab meat, reserve a few pieces to add on top
- 2 red onion, finely chopped
- 2 red bell pepper, finely chopped
- 2 green bell pepper, finely chopped
- 2 cucumber, finely chopped
- olive oil spoons
- For the avocado salad layer:
- 4-6 tablespoons of lemon juice
- Olive oil to taste
- Salt to taste
- Additional accessories:
- pickled onions
- 4-8 radishes, finely chopped
- 4-8 tablespoons finely chopped cilantro
- Juice of 4 small lemons or use 4 large lemon
- Coriander leaves, parsley, etc.

PREPARATION

1 In a large bowl or bowl, combine the cooked crab meat with diced onions, diced bell peppers, diced cucumbers, horseradish, and cilantro.

2 Mix well.

3 Add lemon juice, olive oil and a little salt/pepper to taste.

4 The salad can also be made ahead of time and then kept refrigerated until ready to serve and assemble the avocado and crab layers.

5 For the avocado salad layer:

6 Peel and cut the avocados into squares.

7 Sprinkle with lemon juice, olive oil and salt to taste.

8 The avocado can be diced, thinly sliced, or mashed and pureed for a creamier texture.
9 To assemble and serve the crab and avocado salad layers:
10 Place a lightly oiled round pan in the center of each plate, add the chopped or mashed avocado layer first, gently pressing down to compact as much as possible.
11 Then add a generous layer of the crab salad. Press down and then gently remove the mold.
12 If you save some crab pieces, add them to the top. You can also decorate the salad with coriander leaves and pickled red onions.

RED BEAN SALAD WITH GUACAMOLE

Ingredients

- pinch of pepper
- lemon unit
- pinch of salt
- green pepper unit
- 625 grams of Azuki per pot
- tablespoon of extra virgin olive oil
- fresh Guacamole Frutas Montosa unit can also people 8 minutes
- INGREDIENTS for 8 people
- tomato unit
- onion unit
- red pepper unit
- make it homemade
- small cup of sweet corn in a can

PREPARATION

1 Prepare the salad by mixing all the INGREDIENTS chopped with the previously washed and drained beans.
2 Garnish with lemon juice and oil and season with salt and pepper.
3 Serve the salad with the guacamole and the toast with the toasted bread.

SALAD WITH AVOCADO AND BLACK BEANS

INGREDIENTS

- pinch of balsamic vinegar of Modena
- avocado unit
- pinch of coriander
- chive unit
- pinch of lemon juice
- dash of extra virgin olive oil
- people
- tomato unit
- glass of canned red beans

PREPARATION

1 Divide the avocado and tomato into cubes and the spring onion into thin slices and place in a salad bowl.
2 Add the beans and mix well.
3 Prepare a vinaigrette with lemon juice, vinegar, oil and salt, and sprinkle it on top.
4 Add a little coriander to taste and mix everything.

ASPARAGUS SOUP WITH SALMON

INGREDIENTS

- 640 gr of smoked salmon
- shallots
- fresh chives
- The hand of the croutons
- 455 gr of asparagus
- chicken bouillon cubes
- 400 ml of cream
- 455 gr. flour/cornmeal
- 455 gr. of butter
- fresh parsley to garnish

PREPARATION

1 Cut the asparagus into pieces. Boil for 22 minutes in about 22 liters of water and then cook them for 80 minutes in the water.
2 Finely chop the shallots. Dissolve the butter in a pot and fry the shallots in it. Then add the flour and stir with a whisk to a roux and allow to bake and cook for 22 minutes. Drain the asparagus and collect all the cooking liquid.
3 Dissolve the bouillon cubes in the asparagus cooking liquid.
4 Pour it a little at a time into the roux, continuing to stir with a whisk so that no lumps form.
5 When all the chicken broth has been added, stir in the cream and add the croutons and cooked asparagus.
6 Taste if the soup tastes good and add a pinch of pepper and salt if necessary. Add the salmon strips to the soup. Put the soup on plates and garnish with parsley, salmon and chopped chives.

PUMPKIN GAZPACHO

INGREDIENTS

- tablespoon of vinegar
- pinch of water
- chive unit
- pinch of sea salt
- tablespoon of olive oil extra people
- unit of Ripe Tomatoes
- garlic unit
- 40 grams of pumpkin
- 46 unit of red pepper
- virgin

PREPARATION

1 Grind all the INGREDIENTS until there is a cream, pass them through a strainer and put them in bowls. Serve very cold.

QUINOA AVOCADO SALAD WITH MANGO TOFU CURRY

INGREDIENTS

- For 6 servings
- 280g tofu
- tablespoons of mango juice
- teaspoon curry powder salt pepper
- 280g quinoa

- 86 g sugar chives
- coriander stems
- avocado lime
- tablespoon
- Grape seed oil
- teaspoon of rapeseed oil

PREPARATION

2 Tofu cubes. Mix with 8 tablespoons of mango juice, curry, salt and pepper and leave for about 86 minutes.

3 Meanwhile, wash the quinoa with water and cook it with 4-8 times of salted water for about 46 minutes.

4 Then allow it to cool down. Meanwhile, clean the scab tout, wash and blanch in boiling salted water for 6 minutes, cool, drain and cut in half at an angle.

5 Clean the chives, wash them and cut them into rings. Wash the cilantro, shake it and peel the leaves. Peel and cut the avocado in half, remove the kernel and cut the pulp into small pieces.

6 For the dressing, combine the lime juice with the remaining mango juice, grapeseed oil, salt and pepper and season to taste.

7 Heat the oil in a skillet. Fry the tofu on high heat for 22-24 minutes. Mix the quinoa with all the INGREDIENTS preparations and the dressing, season to taste and serve with the tofu cubes.

SALMON SKEWERS WITH VEGETABLES

INGREDIENTS

- handful of basil 40 g

- 2 organic lemons
- olive oil spoons
- Sea salt
- Pepper
- for 45 pieces
- 2250 g of salmon fillet
- 400g cherry tomatoes
- yellow peppers
- sticks of celery
- garlic cloves
- kitchen appliances
- wooden skewers, 4 barbecue

PREPARATION

1 Rinse salmon under cold water, pat dry, and cut into bite-size cubes.

2 Wash and clean the tomatoes. Wash the peppers, clean them and cut them into pieces.

3 Wash the celery, clean it and cut it into pieces. Alternatively, place the vegetables with the salmon on 45 wooden skewers.

4 Peel the garlic and cut it finely. Wash the basil, shake it to dry it, peel the leaves and chop it.

5 Stir in the garlic, lemon rind, and juice and oil and season with salt and pepper.

6 Brush the skewers on all sides with the oil and cook on the hot grill with regular rotation for about 45 minutes. Brush between times.

Printed in Great Britain
by Amazon

46685473R00076